The Road to Independence

Potty Training Your Special Needs Child

By:

Heather Crafton

For Savannah and Trey, who put me on this path of being a special needs parent. You taught me well. This book is dedicated to all the parents who were told their child would never potty train. May this book pave the way for you. It doesn't matter if your child is 2 or 22, with patience it can be done.

Meet the Family

Savannah was born weighing in at a whopping 11 lbs. 3 oz. She got stuck coming out at birth. The doctor who delivered her, ripped C3-T1 from her spine. This resulted in her being paralyzed on the right side. She has come a long way since then. But this took therapies, many surgeries, and nothing short of miracles. I first had to potty train her. She was very stubborn. Which actually got her farther in life. She would make it to the

bathroom and pee right in front of the toilet

because she struggled getting her pants down

so much. We bought some tools to help her

with zippers, and practiced making it to the

bathroom on time. Even learning to wipe her

bottom was a challenge. And it will be if

your child struggles with fine motor skills.

Trey is our youngest. He was diagnosed with

severe autism at 19 months. At that time, the

doctor gave us a grim outlook. He told us all

the things he would never do and suggested

that we put him in an institution. These

included would never love us, never speak,

never potty train, and have severe aggression.

He is the most loving kid I know. He didn't

really talk until he turned 9. But now uses 2-3

word requests quite a bit. He is very happy

not aggressive. And although it took me 2

full years to complete it totally, he is potty

trained!

Hailey is our oldest. And our Nerotypical

child as commonly used by the autism

community. She is a straight A student, very

social, and plays the cello beautifully.

My husband and I have been happily married

for 20 years. Parenting two special needs kids

was not something we planned on. However,

God has shown us so many wonderful things through our children. They teach us every day, when we take the time to listen. I can't express the importance of learning to laugh at yourself. If you can find a sense of humor, no matter what it is you are facing, the situation will seem so much lighter. We both love the Lord and try to love each other as much.

Personal Statement

First of all let me tell you that in my

experience of having a child diagnosed with

severe autism, your child's readiness and time

table for potty training compared with that of

a typical child may vary vastly. And it will

probably take extra time. I started when my

son turned four, and it took me two full years

to get him to where I could say "He is totally

trained." But talk about life changing! If you

have the patience and endurance to get it

done, it will lead to so, so many more

independent skills that will come through for

your child.

Setting the Stage

The first thing you need to do to begin potty

training is to plan for is the kick-off time

period. I recommend thinking of it as a boot camp, because the first few days really are intense, and you must make a total commitment. You will need a good 3-4 day kick off period to start the intense time period of total potty training focus.

Before involving your child, there are several steps that you must take. Think about your child's interests. Most kids have their own loves and obsessions. You will need this to help get your bathroom child-ready so it will not seem to be a scary place. Bathrooms are often difficult places for kids with special needs. Sounds naturally echo in them; there are smells in bathrooms that aren't present in any other room in the house; and often the lighting seems excessively bright or harsh to these kids. Here are the steps I used.

1. **Get your bathroom child-ready**. When I potty trained my son, he was obsessed with

Veggie Tales. So I printed out all kinds of

Veggie Tales pictures and taped them on the

walls. Knowing pictures of things we liked

would be there helped him want to go in there

more. I also ordered Veggie Tales toys for the

bathroom only. These were new so he was

very interested in them, but he was told that

they were for that room ONLY.

2. **Throw away the pull-ups.** Yes, I know

what you are thinking that I am crazy!

However, this is a necessary step even if it is a messy one.

3. **Buy your child underwear**. Because my child was already a semi-big kid, I just bought white ones. Then I bought iron-ons. I ironed all the Veggie characters to the outside of his underwear. You will be amazed at how much your child really will not want to pee on their favorite characters. Of course, at first they

will, but I would tell him they were sad when they got wet. It does help. Trust me.

4. **Accumulate a basket of toys**. Put in your bathroom a basket of toys that they may only play with while sitting on the potty. This will be a lifesaver in the beginning when they have to sit for a long time. We had books, toys, and even a portable movie player with a new movie only for bathroom time.

5. **Display a visual timer**. This is so important because your child will be able to see for himself how long they must sit on the potty. I made ours myself with sand and 2 Gatorade bottles taped together. We used a three minute timer.

6. **Provide a see-through treat jar that will always be out-of-reach for anyone but the adult doing the potty training**. But you will want to place it where child can see the treats.

Keep reminding them that they will ONLY

get some IF they pee or poop on the potty. We

used Kit Kats because they were easily

divided into sections. I could get 3 servings

out of every bar for him. We also used Dum

Dum suckers. Seeing the treats is highly

motivating! Of course, it was a little

frustrating for the child at first because many

times they will not earn a treat. But I kept

them within his eyesight and kept restating

that he gets a treat IF he pees in the potty.

7. Furnish a warm or weighted lap pad.

This is especially helpful to help with the

poop training. It is soothing and helps with

the tummy pain sometimes associated with

having a bowel movement.

8. Position a small stool in front of the

toilet. My son was very uncomfortable when

his legs would hang down and not touch the floor. By providing the stool, you are giving them a solid foundation on which to place their feet. Just be especially careful with the stool if the child tries to stand up by himself. Since you will be right there with them at all times, the stool should not pose an extra danger.

Potty training 101

The reason it takes 3-4 days of intense training is that for those days, you will need to put your child on the potty every ten minutes. They will sit for 3 minutes at a time, so it is a constant effort. You will need to completely clear your schedule. I had two older children and prepared them by explaining that I would be training their brother and he would need

my almost undivided attention for these days.

They were in first and third grades, so it was

kind of tricky, but I stressed to them how

much they would be helping the process.

As the child you are training gets used to

going on the potty, you can lengthen the time

between placing them on the toilet. When I

took my son up to 20 minutes off on day 2, he

started having pee accidents, so we just

moved back to 10-minute intervals. This took

us a whole week. Remember, this seems like

too much time in the bathroom, but you

WANT them to be successful.

When they do successfully pee or poop in the

potty, make sure you praise them, cheer, and

give them their treat. Let them know how

proud you are of them. Those who have boys

will probably want to start with them sitting

on the potty all the time. This is what I did.

This can be tricky because if they do not hold down their penis you can get peed on. But it was the best way to start for us. He started standing to pee anytime he knew that he did not need to poop after about a year.

A Support Staff

I cannot express enough the importance of having support. This is anyone else who will be spending a lot of time with your child.

Does your child attend day care, spend time with relatives? Is your child in school? If so, you need to have a meeting with all support people to let them know the game plan. Trey had a wonderful teacher who was very supportive and wanted to see him achieve this independence. As an educator, she knows the importance that is has on their overall development. She took him on a schedule at school and gave him the same kit kat rewards we used at home. As well as a lot of praise.

He would not of done as great as he did at

school without the help, love, and support of

Ms. Riley. You can write a potty training

schedule into your childs ARD or IEP as well.

I highly recommend this as it is your legal

document that must be followed.

Night time schedule

You may want to keep your child in pull-ups for night time use only for a while. Or you can stop their fluid intake for at least four hours before bedtime. I did both. I used pull-ups for the first 2 months of potty training because my son was holding his feces all day and would only poop in the pull-ups at first.

After the two months, I purchased water proof

bed pads and kept him in his underwear at

night. He did have the occasional pee

accident, but it helped to speed up the

pooping in the potty. I used the heated pad

for discomfort. You also need to make sure

that your child urinates right before bed and

also upon waking in the morning.

Fear

If your child has special needs and sensory issues, fear is to be expected. I remember my son being very fearful at first. Calming that fear and providing a safe environment is why it is so important to put things in the bathroom that they love and do not have anywhere else in the house. You need them to get

comfortable in there.

Entertainment

Prepare to be very entertaining. I did

everything short of standing on my head to

keep him happy while sitting on the potty.

This is a chance for some creative parenting

skills. We read books, played games, sang

songs over and over, and even watched

movies. It will be so worth it in the grand

scheme of their lives. I kept reminding myself

that we were going to prove the doctors

wrong. And we did.

A word about poop

If your child has sensory issues, chances are

they might smear poop. This is a subject that

is just not talked about. But here goes,

because we need to discuss it. Having a child

who is diagnosed with severe autism means

that I have washed poop off of almost every

surface in my home. It took me a full year to

get him properly poop trained. And during

that time, he pooped on the floor more than

once and made a huge mess with it. I still

watch him to this day so that I can help wipe

his bottom when he poops. I can now proudly

announce he has not smeared his feces in

quite some time. He is a sensory seeker and

always will be. He smells, tastes, and feels everything in his world. So just like when he is around soap that he tries to eat, I make sure someone is with him when he goes to the potty to poop. Flushable wet wipes help a lot with giving them the independence to wipe their bottoms themselves and help them get cleaner than they can with just toilet paper.

These items are a great invention—plan to buy them in bulk!

Working with kids with physical limitations

My daughter was born paralyzed on her right side and unable to walk until the age of 2. So I also have some experience potty training those with physical limitations. If at all possible, dress them in elastic waist pants. Buttons and zippers can be frustrating for anyone. And if you have trouble with fine motor skills, manipulating buttons and zippers can be even more challenging. My daughter used a zipper tool to help her when she did wear clothes with zippers. These days, as a teen, her frustration level is lessening with zippers. My daughter was and is a super stubborn and fiercely independent child. This helped her while she was paralyzed. I would want to run into the bathroom and help her, but she would yell at me that she could do it

and for me to go away. And she had many an

accident in front of the toilet. But I praised her

for making it to the bathroom before having

an accident, and eventually we got through it.

When your child has issues with not

recognizing a sense of urgency to go to the

bathroom, it can make for a longer process.

But it still can be accomplished. Utilizing

reminders to go to the child to go to bathroom

at regular intervals can help somewhat.

Telling you how they need to go potty

There are many ways your child can tell you

that they need to go potty. You can use sign

language, a PECS picture, or words. My son

used PECS to tell us that he had to potty until

he got words at age nine. He now says

"bathroom" and "poop" if he has to go. That

amount of communication makes a world of

difference. The experts said he would never speak, and we are thankful every day for his progress. Before he had words, however, we kept a metal loop with a potty picture on it with us at all times. That way if he had to go potty, he had a way of letting us know when we were out and about. Of course there will be occasional accidents, but just be sure to always carry a change of clothes in your car. This is something that all parents of potty-training kids realize they must do, regardless

of the child's special needs. It's just part of

the process.

Regression, it WILL happen

There is something about illness with our

special needs kids that causes regression. As

with anything our kids do, sometimes there

will be regression, so expect that it will occur.

But also, like in anything else, it does not

mean a failure of the process. It just is a

setback. My son has had this happen several

times over the years. Whenever he has a

stomach bug, we can anticipate regression.

Even adults struggle during this time, so we

need to be extra patient and not be surprised.

Sometimes when the child has accidents, it

can even cause fears of the bathroom to come

back. All this is a process. And within a short

time usually your child will be back on track

and on the road to independence.

Most importantly…

Do NOT give up. I believe that everyone, no

matter how severe their diagnosis or limited

their physical ability, can be potty trained. It

will take loads of patience and probably lots

of time, but do not give up on it. It took me 2

full years to train both of my children with

special needs. It can be very tiring as well as

very challenging. But remember that your

positive approach will rub off on your child

and your expectation of their success with

help them feel like they will be successful.

Potty training is the most important self-help

skill I have given them to this day. It will

improve their self-esteem dramatically and

only increase their confidence and allow more

skills to come out. Thank you for buying this

manual. Happy training!

About the Author

Heather Crafton lives in San Antonio with her husband Terry and her three great kids, two of which have special needs. She loves the Lord and strives to help families like hers who have children with both physical and developmental challenges. Although she lives in Texas now, she was born in Wheeling, West Virginia and will always be a Midwestern girl.

For **I know the plans I have for you**," declares the LORD, "plans to prosper you and not to harm you, plans to give you hope and a future. Jeremiah 29:11.

CPSIA information can be obtained at www.ICGtesting.com
Printed in the USA
LVOW13s2226270414

383484LV00009B/78/P